FUELING THE FUTURE

Nuclear Energy

Elizabeth Raum

Heinemann Library
Chicago, Illinois

Customer Service 888-454-2279

Visit our website at www.heinemannraintree.com

Photo research by Rebecca Sodergren and Hannah Taylor
Illustrations by Jeff Edwards
Designed by Richard Parker and Q2A Solutions
Originated by Chroma Graphics (Overseas) Pte Ltd
Printed and bound in China by Leo Paper Group

12 11 10 09 08
10 9 8 7 6 5 4 3 2 1

Library of Congress Cataloging-in-Publication Data
Raum, Elizabeth.
  Nuclear energy / Elizabeth Raum.
    p. cm. -- (Fueling the future)
  Includes bibliographical references and index.
  ISBN 978-1-4329-1563-6 (hc) -- ISBN 978-1-4329-1569-8 (pb) 1. Nuclear energy--Juvenile
literature. I. Title.
  QC792.5.R38 2008
  333.792'4--dc22
                        2007050770

Acknowledgments
The author and publisher are grateful to the following for permission to reproduce copyright material:
©Alamy pp. 8 (The Print Collector), 12 (Corbis Premium RF), 18 (Directphoto.org); ©Corbis pp. 10 (Hulton-
Deutsch Collection), 21 (Jon Hicks), 25 (epa/Bin Sheng); ©DK Images p. 11 (Clive Streeter); ©Ford Motor
Company Ltd p. 27; ©Getty Images pp. 4 (Photodisc), 16 (Sean Gallup), 17 (Time & Life Pictures), 20 (AFP/
Maxim Kniazkov); ©IAEA p. 22; ©ITER p. 24; ©Lockheadmartin p. 23; ©Panos p. 19 (Gerd Ludwig); ©Still
Pictures pp. 14 (McPHOTO), 15 (sinopictures/CNS/Lug Wang Chun), 6.

Cover photograph of Abstract Image of Radiating Light reproduced with permission of ©Masterfile/Bill
Frymire. Cover background image of blue virtual whirl reproduced with permission of ©istockphoto.com/
Andreas Guskos.

The publishers would like to thank David Hood of the Centre for Alternative Technology for his assistance in
the preparation of this book.

Contents

Some words are shown in bold, **like this**. You can find out what they mean by looking in the glossary.

Where Do We Get Energy?

Energy is the ability to do work or to make things happen. All living things need energy. Plants and animals need energy to grow. People need energy to grow, move, and survive. Learning requires energy, too. We depend on energy to heat and light our homes, and to run factories, schools, and hospitals. We use energy in the form of gasoline to run cars, boats, and airplanes. Much of our energy today comes in the form of electricity. Thanks to electricity, people no longer have to rely directly on the sun for heat and light.

Almost all of the Earth's energy comes from the sun.

Electricity

Energy cannot be made or destroyed, but it can be changed from one form to another. A **power plant** turns one kind of energy into another kind of energy—electricity. Most electric power plants get their energy from **fossil fuels** (oil, natural gas, or coal). Coal is used most often to run electric power plants, especially in Asia. Some electric power plants use energy from flowing water. This is called **hydroelectric power**. Other electric power plants rely on **nuclear energy**.

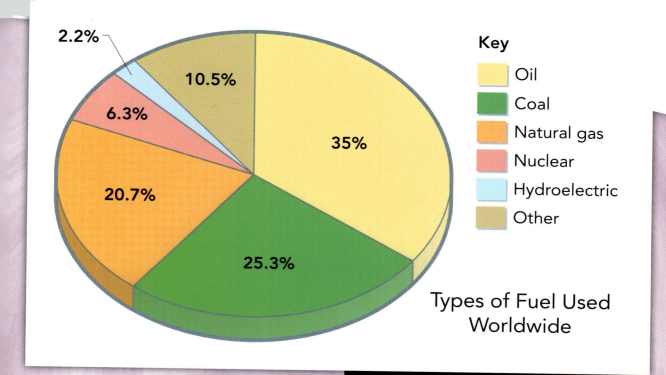

Key
- Oil
- Coal
- Natural gas
- Nuclear
- Hydroelectric
- Other

2.2%

10.5%

6.3%

35%

20.7%

25.3%

Types of Fuel Used Worldwide

As this chart shows, oil is the fuel used most often throughout the world to generate electricity. Coal is second.

Fossil fuels

Fossil fuels run many electric power plants. They also provide the fuel needed to operate cars, trucks, and other vehicles. Fossil fuels were formed millions of years ago from dead plants and animals that were buried under layers of mud and rock. The Earth heated the remains. Shifting rocks buried them even deeper. Over time they changed into oil, natural gas, and coal. When these fuels are burned, they release energy.

Most electric **power plants** use **fossil fuels**, such as coal. Coal provides steady power, but it also **pollutes** (dirties) the air. Burning coal is the leading cause of air pollution in the world today. Coal smoke contains chemicals that are especially dangerous for people with heart or lung problems. Air pollution hurts everyone, but it is especially harmful for older people and young children.

Power plants using coal send dangerous chemicals into the air.

Global warming

Many scientists also blame fossil fuels for **global warming**. Fossil fuels release **carbon dioxide** and other **greenhouse gases** into the **atmosphere**. Over time this may increase the temperature of the Earth, causing global warming. Many people worry that global warming will change the Earth's climate (weather pattern). Too much rain or not enough rain could cause serious problems.

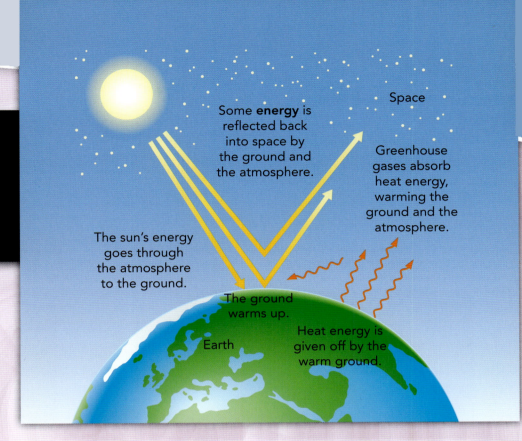

Some **energy** is reflected back into space by the ground and the atmosphere.

Space

Greenhouse gases absorb heat energy, warming the ground and the atmosphere.

The sun's energy goes through the atmosphere to the ground.

The ground warms up.

Earth

Heat energy is given off by the warm ground.

Carbon is found in all living things. In fact, without carbon there would not be life on Earth. Carbon makes up part of a gas called carbon dioxide. Plants and animals release carbon dioxide into the air when they breathe. There is carbon dioxide in animal and plant waste. Carbon dioxide and other natural chemicals help keep the Earth warm by trapping the sun's energy in the Earth's atmosphere. This is called the **greenhouse effect**. Burning fossil fuels releases extra greenhouse gases into the atmosphere. This causes the problem of global warming.

Finding alternative energy

World leaders and scientists are working together to find **alternative** (different) energy sources that will not pollute the Earth or add to the problem of global warming. **Nuclear energy** is one of the possible choices.

What Is Nuclear Energy?

Nuclear energy is **energy** produced by splitting **atoms**. Atoms are the tiny building blocks that make up all things. Everything is made of atoms, but it takes billions of atoms to make things like desks, bicycles, animals, or people.

In 1911 Ernest Rutherford, a scientist from New Zealand, discovered the nucleus of an atom. In 1920 he proved that atoms could be split apart.

Atoms

Atoms are made of a center, called a **nucleus**, that is surrounded by **electrons**. The nucleus itself is made up of **particles** called **neutrons** and **protons**. It takes enormous energy to hold the neutrons and protons together. When the nucleus of an atom is split apart, it releases that energy. This energy is called nuclear (from the nucleus) energy. It can be used to make electricity. The kind of nuclear energy in use today comes from nuclear **fission** (splitting atoms).

The process of splitting atoms is complex. Scientists called **physicists** began to understand nuclear energy by accident. Each physicist built on the earlier work of other physicists who had made important discoveries. Over time they came to understand atoms and how to use their energy.

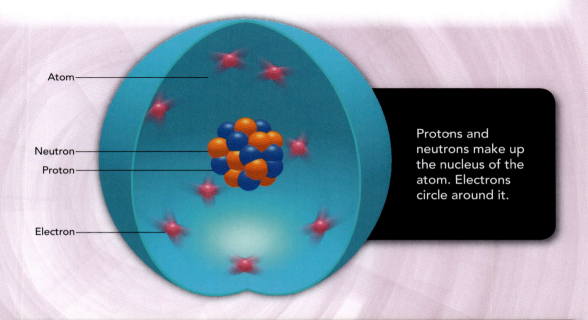

Atom

Neutron

Proton

Electron

Protons and neutrons make up the nucleus of the atom. Electrons circle around it.

Steps to discovery

By 1920 physicists had discovered that an atom has protons packed closely together in its center and electrons outside the nucleus. In 1932 James Chadwick, a British physicist, suggested that there must be another particle in the nucleus. He called it the neutron. Italian physicist Enrico Fermi experimented with neutrons. German physicists Otto Hahn and Fritz Strassmann put all this research together. In 1938 they discovered that if a neutron strikes a nucleus, the nucleus will break apart, releasing energy and two or three more neutrons. This splitting apart is called fission.

Uranium

In 1789 a German chemist named Martin Klaproth discovered **uranium**. A friend suggested he name the new **element** "klaprothium," but Klaproth chose to call it "uranium" after the planet Uranus. Uranium is a heavy metal used to produce nuclear energy. In 1895 Wilhelm Roentgen, a German physicist, discovered an invisible energy. He didn't know what it was, so he called it X (or unknown) rays. This powerful energy, which can pass through solid objects, comes from uranium.

Henri Becquerel, a scientist working in France, also studied this invisible energy. Marie Curie and her husband, Pierre, continued Becquerel's work and called the energy **radioactivity**. They won important scientific awards for their work.

Marie Curie spent years studying uranium samples to learn about radiation.

Energy from uranium

When physicists first tried to split atoms, they chose to work with uranium. When the uranium atoms were split, they released enormous amounts of heat. Scientists began planning how to use the heat from fission for energy. They discovered that a particular form of uranium, known as U-235, works best for providing energy.

Uranium mining

Uranium **ore** is found underground. Canada, Australia, Kazakhstan (in central Asia), and Russia are the biggest producers of uranium used in nuclear power today. In the future, mining companies may turn to Africa as another source of uranium.

After miners dig the uranium ore out of the ground, they crush it and grind it up. Then they send the uranium to scientists who remove a kind of uranium called U-235. The U-235 is used to make nuclear energy.

This brownish-black rock contains uranium.

Radiation

Uranium gives off waves, or rays, called **radiation**. Anyone working with uranium must wear special gloves and clothing as protection. Large amounts of radiation may cause cancer and other illnesses.

How Does Nuclear Energy Work?

Scientists use a machine called a **particle accelerator** to split the **atoms** in U-235. The particle accelerator shoots **neutrons** into the **nucleus** of an atom of U-235. The nucleus splits, releasing more heat and more neutrons. Those neutrons fly off, splitting more atoms apart. This releases even more heat and more neutrons. This is called a **chain reaction**. It's similar to what happens when you knock down the first domino in a row of standing dominoes. One domino hits another, and then another, until the entire row of dominoes has fallen over.

The big difference between dominoes and a nuclear chain reaction is that a nuclear chain reaction is so powerful that it must be carefully controlled. Modern **nuclear power plants** are built to control and use chain reactions.

The dome-shaped building is the containment building for this nuclear power plant in England.

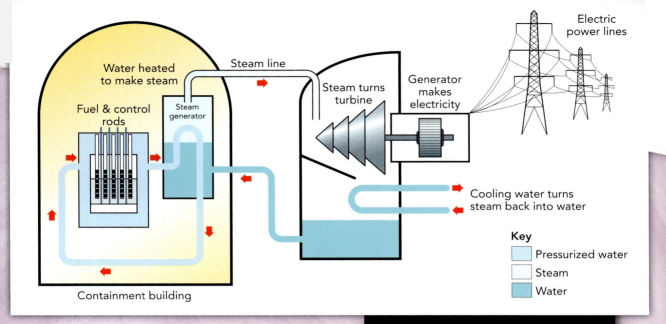

This diagram shows how electricity is generated in a nuclear power plant.

Labels in diagram:
Electric power lines
Water heated to make steam
Steam line
Steam turns turbine
Generator makes electricity
Fuel & control rods
Steam generator
Cooling water turns steam back into water
Containment building

Key
Pressurized water
Steam
Water

Nuclear power plants

A nuclear power plant uses the heat released by nuclear **fission** to make steam. The steam spins the blades of a machine called a **turbine**, which sends energy to a **generator**. This machine generates (makes) electricity. Power lines carry the electricity to homes, schools, and businesses.

In today's nuclear power plants, the nuclear reaction occurs inside a **containment building** that has concrete and steel walls 3 feet (1 meter) thick. The walls protect people outside from the uranium used in generating nuclear power. **Physicists** use cold water and control rods to prevent the chain reaction from getting out of control. For this reason, most power plants are located near an ocean, river, or lake. The water is needed to make steam and to cool the **reactor**. Some nuclear power plants have more than one reactor.

World's largest nuclear power plant

The Kashiwazaki nuclear plant in Japan is the largest in the world. It has seven nuclear reactors and supplies electricity to 16 million homes.

At first, **nuclear energy** was used to build powerful bombs. Two huge nuclear bombs were dropped on Japan in 1945 at the end of World War II (1939–1945). The power of the nuclear explosion stunned the world. After the war, **physicists** began developing peaceful uses for nuclear energy. At the time, England needed fuel for its growing factories. Nuclear energy seemed a good choice. The world's first **nuclear power plant** opened in 1956, in northern England.

Both the United States and Russia (then called the Soviet Union) opened nuclear power plants soon after. Nuclear energy grew quickly in the 1970s and early 1980s. By 1987 almost 16 percent of the world's electricity came from nuclear energy. At first most nuclear power plants were built in Europe and North America.

Calder Hall, a nuclear power plant, opened in 1956 in northern England.

Asia, South America, and Africa

Countries in Asia, South America, and Africa need more energy now than in the past. Many are considering nuclear energy. South America, Argentina, Chile, and Brazil plan to build up to five nuclear plants each. South Korea gets more than 38 percent of its electricity from nuclear sources. In Japan, 30 percent of the electricity used is nuclear. Taiwan now gets 22 percent of its electricity from nuclear power.

These countries are choosing nuclear energy because their energy needs are growing rapidly, and they do not have reserves of **fossil fuels**. Nuclear energy provides a clean, reliable **alternative**.

More energy in less space

Experts say that it would take 16,000 **wind turbines** to produce as much energy as Japan's Kashiwazaki nuclear power plant produces each day. The biggest wind farm in the world today has fewer than 200 wind turbines.

Reliable energy

Nuclear energy provides steady and reliable energy. Unlike wind energy and **solar energy** that need windy or sunny days, nuclear energy provides electricity no matter what the weather.

In 2006, the German chancellor, Angela Merkel, and the then French president, Jacques Chirac, met to discuss nuclear energy.

Clean energy

Nuclear energy does not cause air pollution. Canada plans to build 12 nuclear power plants to replace power plants using coal. France, which gets 78 percent of its electricity from nuclear energy, has five times less air pollution than it had before using nuclear energy. This is one reason that countries in Asia, South America, and Africa are looking to nuclear power.

The *Nautilus*, launched in 1954, was the world's first nuclear-powered submarine.

Nature or nuclear?

World leaders worried about **global warming** are also turning to nuclear energy. Several new nuclear power plants are being built in Europe. The United States and the United Kingdom are considering building more nuclear power plants.

In 2002 Germany decided to close all 19 of its nuclear power plants by 2020 because of safety concerns. They planned to rely on **renewable** energy sources like wind, water, and solar energy. However, when Germany's new chancellor, Angela Merkel, took office, she urged Germany to return to nuclear energy. Nuclear energy will help Germany meet its energy needs without adding to global warming.

Nuclear submarines

Navies of the United States, France, and the United Kingdom use nuclear-powered submarines. A nuclear **reactor** built into the submarine supplies the energy that moves the ship. It also provides energy needed for daily living. The reactor can make oxygen and pure water from seawater. Nuclear energy allows the submarines to spend months underwater without refueling.

Many people worry about the dangers of **nuclear energy**. An accident at a nuclear **reactor** could release **radiation**. Exposure to radiation causes cancer and other health problems. Several accidents have occurred in the past.

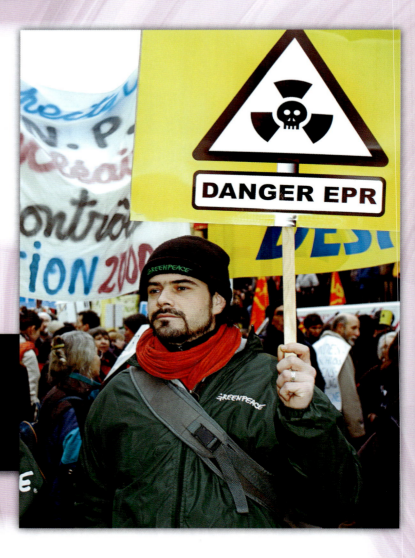

These people want to stop the building of nuclear power plants.

Three Mile Island

In 1979 there was an accident at Three Mile Island **nuclear power plant** in Pennsylvania. Workers shut down the reactor quickly. Many people left the area because they were afraid that radiation had escaped into the **atmosphere**. Some wanted the government to shut down all nuclear power plants and to stop building new ones. They felt the danger of nuclear accidents was too great.

Chernobyl

In 1986 an accident occurred at the Chernobyl nuclear power plant in the Ukraine (southwest of Russia). One reactor exploded and broke out in flames. Workers and firefighters were exposed to radiation. Experts disagree about how many people have died of illnesses caused by the accident. Some claim 9,000 people have died or will die. Others put the number closer to 100,000. Scientists discovered that the reactor was poorly designed. They also found that poorly trained workers did not follow safety rules.

After the nuclear accident, everyone left Chernobyl.

Could it happen again?

Some experts believe that new safety rules and better reactors make it unlikely that another accident like Chernobyl will happen. Others say that because people make mistakes it could happen again. In 2007 an earthquake in Japan caused a fire in a nuclear power plant there. Some radiation escaped during the fire, but it did not cause any major damage. Accidents like these are frightening. Many people do not want nuclear power plants built near their homes.

Nuclear waste

Nuclear power plants produce nuclear waste. Used nuclear fuel is radioactive. Nuclear waste does not decay (break down) for thousands of years, so it must be stored in special containers and buried deep underground. The United States is building an underground storage site in the Nevada desert at Yucca Mountain. It will be finished in 2010. Until then, most nuclear waste is stored at the plants where it was made.

Even though Japan, Russia, and the United Kingdom plan to safely recycle (use again) their nuclear waste, there will still be some waste material to bury underground.

The United States is building a nuclear waste dump at Yucca Mountain in Nevada.

Terrorism

The **uranium** that is used to produce electricity can also be used to make bombs. Some people fear that terrorists could make bombs from supplies set aside for use in nuclear power plants. Others fear that terrorists will target nuclear power plants. By destroying a nuclear reactor, they could release radiation into the air.

These brightly painted cooling towers are part of a nuclear power plant in South Africa.

Cost

Nuclear reactors are expensive to build. A new nuclear power plant costs up to three times more than a plant that runs on **fossil fuels**. Taking care of nuclear waste is costly, too. However, once a nuclear power plant is built, the cost to generate electricity is less expensive than using fossil fuels.

Is there enough uranium?

Uranium, which is used to make nuclear energy, is not a **renewable** source. Someday it will run out. However, experts believe that the current supply of uranium will last 50 to 65 years. It may be possible to recycle uranium. Scientists also hope to find ways to remove traces of uranium from seawater and use it in nuclear reactors.

In 2000 several countries began working together to research new **nuclear power plant** systems. Argentina, Brazil, Canada, France, Japan, South Africa, South Korea, Switzerland, the United Kingdom, and the United States began the project. They asked China and Russia to join them. The group is called the Generation IV International Forum.

Reactors now in use are called third-generation reactors. The new systems will be called Generation IV. They will have shorter construction times and cost less than the third-generation reactors. This will make **nuclear energy** more affordable for poorer countries. Scientists will work together to increase reactor safety and prevent nuclear terrorism. Generation IV nuclear power plants will make less nuclear waste by reusing nuclear fuel. New reactors will also last for up to 60 years. Many countries are replacing older reactors with newer models.

This new nuclear power plant is being built in Japan.

Nuclear energy will speed this spacecraft on its journey to Pluto.

Other uses

Nuclear **physicists** continue to find new uses for nuclear energy. Nuclear energy is already used in submarines, ships, and spacecrafts. In the future, airplanes and cars may use **energy** generated by nuclear power plants instead of oil or natural gas.

Nuclear energy in space

For years, scientists have debated the use of nuclear energy in space. Russian spacecraft have used nuclear energy for years. In 2006 the United States launched a nuclear reactor in its *New Horizons* spacecraft. *New Horizons* is scheduled to reach Pluto in 2015. A nuclear reactor on board will power the spacecraft during its nine-year trip. Using nuclear energy allows the spacecraft to travel 36,000 miles (58,000 kilometers) per hour.

What is nuclear fusion?

Today nuclear physicists are working on a new kind of nuclear energy. It is called nuclear **fusion**. "Nuclear **fission**" is the term scientists use to describe the process of splitting **atoms** apart. Nuclear fusion is the opposite. Fusion is what happens when atoms combine to make a heavier **nucleus**. The sun gets its energy from nuclear fusion. Extremely high temperatures fuse (combine) nuclei together. Nuclear fusion provides much greater energy than nuclear fission.

It takes a great deal of energy to create temperatures high enough to cause nuclear fusion. Scientists are learning how to control these high temperatures. Some experts predict that energy from fusion will be possible in 30–40 years.

This drawing shows how the new ITER center in France will look after it is built.

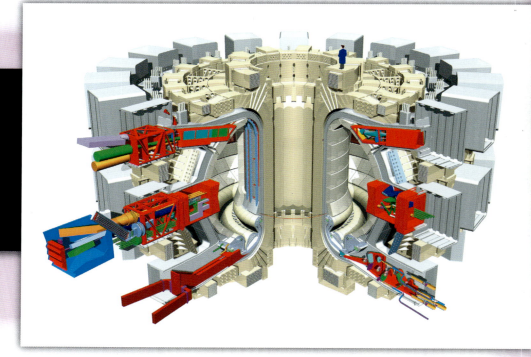

ITER

ITER is the name of an international project started in 1985 to develop energy from nuclear fusion. Scientists in Europe, Asia, and the United States are trying to find ways to use fusion for energy.

Fusion is one of the most powerful reactions in the world. But it is not easy to control. In 2005 ITER chose France as the site of its research center. The center will soon be under construction. Scientists from around the world will work with a $6 billion fusion reactor called a tokamak.

These Chinese scientists are working with a tokamak reactor.

Water as fuel

Fusion will not use **uranium** as fuel. It will use a substance called deuterium, which is found in water. There will be no risk of nuclear accidents or nuclear waste. Fusion will not **pollute** the air or add **greenhouse gases**.

Is fusion possible? Scientists around the world think so. But it will take years before we know for certain whether fusion is the energy of the future.

What's the Future of Nuclear Energy?

It's been less than 100 years since Otto Hahn and Fritz Strassmann first showed the world how nuclear **fission** works. In that time, **physicists** have invented nuclear **reactors** and designed **nuclear power plants**. Today over one billion people get their electricity from nuclear power plants. **Nuclear energy** provides a strong, steady power that does not **pollute** or add to **global warming**.

However, many people worry about the dangers of nuclear energy. Thousands of people in the Ukraine still suffer the effects of the accident at Chernobyl. Even though there are better safety rules now, an accident could happen. Is nuclear energy worth the risk?

Many countries have decided that it is. Today the United States is expanding its nuclear energy program by building more nuclear power plants and repairing older plants to keep them running.

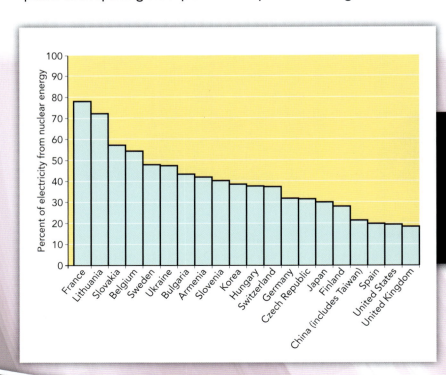

This chart shows the percentage of electricity that each country receives from nuclear energy.

Planning ahead

Scientists continue to work on new energy ideas. Maybe nuclear fusion will be the fuel of the future. Maybe the best answer will be to combine more than one type of **energy**. Some Canadian scientists suggest that using both wind power and nuclear energy together may be the best way to make **hydrogen**, a fuel used to run hydrogen cars.

For now, countries have to make difficult decisions. World leaders want to cut back on the use of **fossil fuels**. What other energy sources will they use? Is nuclear energy a good choice?

Wind and nuclear energy may work together to provide the fuel for this hydrogen car.

Hydrogen cars

Hydrogen cars run on a hydrogen fuel cell, a kind of battery. Hydrogen, like nuclear energy, does not pollute the air or add to global warming. The first hydrogen cars are now in use. However, there are very few hydrogen fuel stations.

This map shows the location of **nuclear power plants** throughout the world. Most nuclear power plants are in North America and Europe. There are far fewer in Africa, Asia, or South America. But the **energy** needs of these countries are growing. Plans are underway to build more nuclear power plants in these areas.

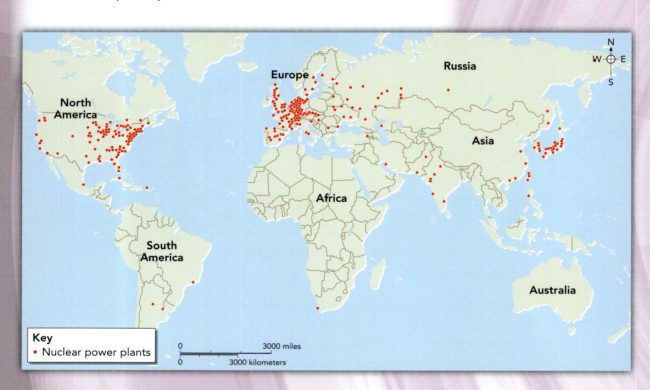

Key
• Nuclear power plants

0   3000 miles

0   3000 kilometers

Nuclear Energy Timeline

1789   Martin Klaproth, a German chemist, discovers **uranium.**

1895   Wilhelm Roentgen discovers X-rays.

1896   Marie and Pierre Curie discover **radioactivity**.

1898   Marie and Pierre Curie discover radium.

1934   Enrico Fermi makes a breakthrough in understanding nuclear power.

1938   Otto Hahn and Fritz Strassmann demonstrate nuclear **fission.**

1942   Enrico Fermi demonstrates a nuclear **chain reaction.**

1945   Nuclear weapons are used on Hiroshima and Nagasaki.

1954   U.S.S. *Nautilus*, the first nuclear submarine, is launched.

1956   First **nuclear** power plant begins operating in the United Kingdom.

1962   First ship to run on **nuclear energy** is launched.

1979   Three Mile Island Nuclear Power plant near Harrisburg, Pennsylvania, suffers a partial meltdown.

1986   Chernobyl Nuclear Reactor in the Ukraine suffers a meltdown. Radioactive waste is released into the air.

1991   China completes its first nuclear power plant.

1996   United Nations approves a ban on nuclear weapon testing.

2000   Generation IV International Forum meets to consider the future of nuclear energy.

2002   Germany decides to close all nuclear power plants by 2020; U.S. Congress approves Yucca Mountain in Nevada as a disposal site for nuclear waste.

2005   France is chosen as the site of the ITER research center.

2006   *New Horizons* spacecraft leaves for Pluto powered by on-board nuclear **reactor**.

2007   Earthquake in Japan damages nuclear power plant.

2008   Over 440 nuclear power plants provide electricity worldwide. People continue to debate the use of nuclear energy.

Glossary

alternative   new or different

atmosphere   layer of gases that surround the Earth

atom   small building block of all matter

atomic   having to do with atoms

carbon   natural element that is necessary to all life

carbon dioxide   greenhouse gas released when fossil fuels are burned. It is a colorless gas breathed out by animals and absorbed from the air by plants.

chain reaction   event that sets off other events

containment building   strong building designed to hold a nuclear reactor

electron   particle that circles the nucleus of an atom

element   substance made of only one kind of atom

energy   ability to do work

fission   process that releases energy by splitting the nucleus of an atom

fossil fuel   fuel formed millions of years ago from decayed plants and animals

fusion   process that releases energy by combining the nucleus of an atom with the nucleus of another atom

generator   machine that changes one kind of energy into another, such as nuclear energy into electricity

global warming   increase in temperature of the Earth's land and water

greenhouse effect   rise in temperature on the Earth because certain gases trap energy from the sun

greenhouse gas   type of gas that traps the Earth's heat in the atmosphere. Greenhouse gases include water vapor, carbon dioxide, and methane.

hydroelectric power   electricity that comes from water

hydrogen   colorless, odorless, flammable gas that can be used as a fuel

neutron   particle in the nucleus of an atom

nuclear energy   energy made by splitting atoms

nuclear power plant   factory that makes electricity from nuclear energy

nucleus   the center of an atom; the plural is "nuclei"

ore   type of rock in which metals such as uranium can be found

particle   extremely small piece

particle accelerator   machine used to shoot neutrons into a nucleus

physicist   scientist who studies what things are made of and how they work

pollute   make dirty or unclean

power plant   factory that makes electricity

proton   particle in the nucleus of an atom

radiation   process in which energy is emitted (given out) as particles or waves

radioactivity   release of radiation by atomic nuclei

reactor   place where nuclear fission takes place

renewable   describes something that can replace itself over time

turbine   engine or machine that changes one form of energy to another (often electricity)

uranium   heavy metal used as fuel in nuclear power plants

wind turbine   engine or machine that captures energy from the wind

Find Out More

Books

McLeish, Ewan. *Energy Resources: Our Impact on the Planet*. Austin, Texas: Raintree , 2002.

Morris, Neil. *Nuclear Power*. North Mankato, Minn.: Smart Apple Media, 2006.

Scarborough, Kate. *Nuclear Waste*. Mankato, Minn.: Capstone, 2003.

Parker, Steve. *Nuclear Energy*. Milwaukee: Gareth Stevens, 2003.

Sneddon, Robert. *Nuclear Energy*. Chicago: Heinemann Library, 2006.

Websites

Energy Quest Games
www.energyquest.ca.gov/games/index.html

Energy Kids' Page
www.eia.doe.gov/kids/energyfacts/sources/whatsenergy.html

Get Close to a Nuclear Fission Reaction!
www.pbs.org/wgbh/pages/frontline/shows/reaction/interact/getclose.html

Nuclear World
www.aecl.ca/kidszone/atomicenergy/nuclear/index.asp

Index